Thank God
I Grew Up
in
Chowchilla

Acknowledgements

Thank you to:

Traja Rosenthal for editing suggestions and Roberta Zanganeh for research assistance and editing suggestions

Ellen Wessels Nicks for copyright permission to use photos taken by her late father, George Wessels

Craig and Linda Johnson for production advice

Krista Beck, Rev. Walter M. Sutherland's great-granddaughter, and Leslie Vaughn, Rev. Sutherland's granddaughter, for submitting family pictures

Betsy Fry Hofer for submitting newspaper articles from her family albums

Marty Piepenbrok, Community Relations Manager, City of Chowchilla, for his research and assistance

The McClatchy Corporation and Gold Country Media for copyright permissions

Pastor Ralph Supper of the Lutheran Church of the Resurrection for photo permission

Lutheran Church of the Resurrection member Josie Freiberg for photo permission

Created by CreateSpace

ISBN #978-1979927437

Printed in the United States of America

". . .it's passionately interesting to me that the things I learned in a small town, in a very modest home, are just the things that I believe have won the election."

Margaret Thatcher (1925-2013), Prime Minister of Great Britain
1979-1990

My mother, Florence Shobe, and I in front of our family home on Robertson Boulevard in Chowchilla in 1984.

Introduction

Borrowing from an African proverb, "It takes a village to raise a child," and later Hillary Clinton's book, *It Takes a Village,* I grew up in a "village." A village could be any town or city in the United States or in any other country. However, for me it was Chowchilla, California, a small agricultural San Joaquin Valley town, where I lived from 1946 until 1963. This book gives glimpses into my village.

For many years, when I told people the name of my hometown, I often was met with "Isn't that the name of some dog (a chow {a dog} or a chinchilla, which is really a type of rodent)?" And then, after the tragic, world-publicized Chowchilla school bus kidnapping in 1976, the response usually was something like, "Oh yes, that's where they had the bus-kidnapping."

To the earlier "dog" question, I responded, "I'm quite sure Chowchilla was named after an Indian tribe that once lived in the area." (Wikipedia gives the name as Chauchila) .

4

To the bus-kidnapping response, I would respond that the whole community was shocked that an act extremely hurtful to children could have happened in our peaceful, bucolic community, but also that the community immediately came together to embrace the children, their families, and the bus driver.

That was Chowchilla, my village as I remembered it.

Now, even though over the years I have "mentally photoshopped" my life in my small hometown to create a picture of an idyllic childhood, during the past few months I have disciplined myself to view those years as filled with unedited "snapshots." And, like unidentified pictures in old photo albums, my memory snapshots, I knew, would have no meaning for me or for anyone else unless they could result in new villages.

This book is about a few of the memory snapshots I have chosen to keep (The quotes I cite are as I remember them):

Stephens School originally was Chowchilla Grammar School, built in 1913.

Memory Snapshot #1: My first day of school at Stephens School in Chowchilla

"Hi, I'm Nicky."

Veronica Wadewitz, student Stephens School

**Veronica
"Nicky"
Wadewitz**

**Dianne Shobe
Age 7**

Because I had started kindergarten midyear in Modesto, California, I was 6 years old, a half-year behind the other second-grade students when I enrolled in Stephens School in Chowchilla. I was terrified when my mother dropped me off the first day of school. I was the stranger in a room full of children. The teacher introduced me to the class as a new student, but, as I recall, did nothing to make me feel welcome. The students merely stared as I walked to an empty seat. I dreaded the first school recess, the time when students usually ran out of the room laughing and starting to play games. However, right after the recess bell rang and the teacher dismissed us for the short break, a blond, pigtailed classmate walked to my desk.

"Hi, I'm Nicky," she said. "Come on outside with me."

Over the years

Nicky also invited me to go to Sunday School with her at Chowchilla's First Presbyterian Church, which was located on Trinity Street. And, although the only activities that drew us together in Chowchilla were our church activities — such as Christian Endeavor, the high school group — and the elementary school and high school bands, Nicky and I remained good friends throughout our school years.

After high school and college, we kept in touch mostly through Christmas cards. She married, had two children and then divorced. Fortunately, at a party at my widowed mother's Chowchilla home several years later, she reunited with one of our Chowchilla classmates, Dr. Stanley Crouch, a chemistry professor at Michigan State University. They immediately fell in love, married and, thankfully, had several good years together before Nicky became seriously ill and died in her mid-70s in Santa Rosa.

An empty chair at a freshman assembly my first day at the College of the Pacific (Yes, it was not the University of the Pacific then) resulted in an "Hi, I'm Nicky" friendship that has lasted almost 60 years. I was fortunate to sit in the empty chair next to Julia Kay Harris, a friend so special that my husband and I named our daughter, Julie, after her. My most vivid memory of my new friend's thoughtfulness: She and I were on our way to the laundry room when a girl in our hall handed Julie a laundry basket and asked her to get her clothes out of the dryer and bring them back up to her. I would have found the clothes and thrown them into the basket. However, Julie folded them and put them in the basket while she and I waited for our clothes to dry.

Fortunately me, Julie and her husband, Hal Morton, retired to Roseville and live about 10 minutes from my home.

In elementary school, high school, college, the workplace and in the area in which I have lived 45 years, I have made friendships that have lasted and grown more treasured throughout the years. For all of them I am grateful.

Even though I had not seen Nicky for several years, as her longtime friend, hostess of the dinner that brought Nicky and Stan together and the matron of honor at their Fresno wedding, I was asked to join Nicky's family for the scattering of her ashes at Bodega Bay, a favorite place of

Nicky and Stan's because it was a vacation area on the Pacific Ocean not far from their Santa Rosa home.

I have no idea what image of Nicky each family member remembered as the wife, sister, mother and grandmother's ashes were strewn in the ocean, but, for me, the woman whose death I was mourning was a little girl with blond pigtails.

Memory Snapshot #2: The Chowchilla High School Band

O wad some Power the giftie gie us
To see oursels as ithers see us!"

From "To a Louse; On Seeing One on a Lady's Bonnet at Church,"
by Robert Burns, Scottish poet

From 1945 to 1953, the CUHS Marching Band, under the direction of Ralph Bredenberg, was a prize-winning Chowchilla treasure. Music students sought the envied chairs in each section of the band. The organization regularly garnered trophies at the All-Western Band Review in Long Beach and took home honors in nearly every parade to which it was invited. When the Chowchilla High School Band marched down the street, it was welcomed by loud applause.

After Mr. Bredenberg moved on to a bigger band in a bigger city, the Chowchilla band, under a new director, began to lose its luster and continued to march in the glory of its imagination. After all, it was the Chowchilla Union High School Band.

During the summer of 1954, when I joined the band, the new director challenged the band to learn Sousa's "Stars and Stripes Forever" in preparation for the annual Long Beach review parade in November. He reminded us that a band as good as ours should be playing a challenging piece for the review judges, and we practiced the Sousa piece with the vision of bringing the event's trophy to our hometown.

Then, at the beginning of the school year, word spread that our new director had vanished. School officials were mum. Rumors flew. Band members, boys and girls alike, sobbed. Where was he? What director in

10

George Wessels photography, with permission of his daughter, Ellen Wessels Nicks, published in the 1958 La Entrada

The 1957-58 Chowchilla High School Band, under the direction of Herbert L. Stephens, shown in front of the band room at Chowchilla High School.

his right mind would abandon OUR band. We were devastated. The final word, though, was that he definitely was gone, that there would be no explanation, and that he would not be back. That was that. Not giving up on our trip to Long Beach, however, the older members of the band began to spread the word that we would practice without him, travel to the competition and, without a doubt, bring home the big trophy. Wherever our former director was, he would hear and be proud.

After a short time, Neal Wade, our school principal, walked into the band room with a man quite a bit older than our former director and introduced him as our new director, Herbert L. Stephens. An uncomfortable silence followed. Our former director was rather young. Mr. Stephens looked old (He probably was in his early 50s, but to teens that was not "cool."). Our former director wore jeans and T-shirts. Mr. Stephens was in a brown suit. Our former director was a lot of fun, made us laugh, Mr. Stephens' eyes showed no hint of humor.

Then it got worse. Mr. Stephens took the podium, told us to put "The Stars and Stripes Forever" back into our folders, and said, with quiet authority. "You are not ready to play that piece -- and you won't be ready in time for the Long Beach parade."

From the Shobe family collection

Herbert L. Stephens, Chowchilla High School band director

Was he serious? Who did this obvious outsider think he was? Where had Mr. Wade found him, and what was he thinking when he hired this man? We were, to say the least, incensed and, no doubt, let Mr. Stephens know it by rolling our eyes and slamming our folders shut.

Mr. Stephens then distributed a very simple band piece and told us that we would be learning it for the Long Beach review. We were insulted. Were we honestly going to Long Beach, put on our beautiful red and white band uniforms, march behind our prize-winning majorettes and drum major, and play a song more suited to our town's elementary school band?

Mr. Stephens did not stop there. He announced that sections of the band would be meeting with him at 7 a.m. weekly and that members who did not show up for the sectionals would be dropped from the band. We hated having to get to school an hour early. We complained loudly behind his back. However, all members of the band grudgingly showed up for the early-morning sessions. I played the clarinet in the marching band

and the oboe when our band was in concert. For our clarinet section, he immediately took away our "inferior" soft reeds and made us play on very hard reeds in order to get a better tone. At first, no matter how hard we blew into our wooden clarinets, we could get only a puffed bleat out of our instruments, but we got better and better. He also made the players of all the wind instruments and horns strengthen our embouchures, the way our mouths fit around our mouthpieces. He watched our mouths individually as we played. He was relentless. Gradually, the clarinetists began to create music on our new reeds and our embouchures strengthened.

That first year, we marched down the streets of Long Beach to weak applause, and we did not place in our division. We were disheartened and secretly blamed our director for not letting us play "The Stars and Stripes Forever." Mr. Stephens was not fazed.

When we returned to Chowchilla, we started preparing for our concert season, specifically for a spring regional band review at which we would receive judges' written ratings of our performance. Mr. Stephens continued our mandatory morning sectionals and his demand for hard reeds and better embouchures.

On the day of the review, which was in Clovis, California, a few parents and a scattering of music lovers attended the high school band performances prior to ours. However, at our band's performance time, as we sat on the stage, the curtain opened to an auditorium with no empty seats. Our band was greeted with loud applause before Mr. Stephens came on stage to take the podium. FINALLY, we thought (and even mentioned to each other), Mr. Stephens will see the packed house and understand how much our band is respected throughout our part of the San Joaquin Valley and we, no doubt, FINALLY will get the respect we deserve from him.

And then, as Mr. Stephens walked onto the stage, the entire audience immediately rose to give HIM an ovation that seemed to last more than two minutes. WHAT??? THE AUDIENCE WASN'T THERE FOR US? WHAT IS THIS? Quickly, though, word traveled throughout the band, "Remember, Mr. Stephens was a band director in this area before he came to us."

After briefly acknowledging the sustained applause, Mr. Stephens took the podium, faced our band and raised his arms to begin our performance. No smug smile, no subtle reference to his reception. And, following our performance, which, too, elicited loud applause, he extended his arm to our band in recognition of our performance.

At that moment, our band wanted everyone in the audience to know that Mr. Stephens was OUR director.

Over the years

By 1957. the Chowchilla Union High School Band, under the direction of Herbert L. Stephens, was rated Superior in playing and sight-reading in the central section of the Music Educators National Conference Music Festival, First Place in the Los Banos May Day Parade and First in its class at the All-Western Band Review in Long Beach. Interestingly, but not surprisingly, several of the event judges mentioned our band's excellent tone.

Mr. Stephens died in his 60s after minor surgery. I remember him with fondness and deep respect.

Memory Snapshot No. 3: A Short Conversation
With My Mother

"Sure, but you'll be singing in the church choir this Sunday."

My mother, Florence Garrison Shobe
(1912-2002)

While I was away from home one summer morning during my high school years, a girl phoned to see if she could come to our home for the afternoon. I knew the girl only through Job's Daughters, a young women's organization related to the Masons, and did not think of her as one of

**My mother,
Florence Shobe**

my good friends. When I arrived home, Mother told me the girl had called and urged me to call the girl and invite her over. When I responded that I really did not want to spend the afternoon with the girl, my mother merely said, "Sure, but you'll be singing in the church choir this Sunday."

I should have known that her response was what I was going to hear. No lecture, no begging me to call the girl, just that. Her response alone was a powerful sermon. I called the girl and invited her over, not because I suddenly was a better person. No, I had to live with Florence Shobe.

I do not remember my mother ever hugging me, kissing me, telling me that she loved me. She also was short on praise. (After a piano recital, in which, as an eighth-grader, I had played "The Warsaw Concerto" -- very well, I thought -- I was waiting for some verbal applause from my mother. "You played very well," she said. "So did the other students."

On the other hand, when my parents became part-owners of the Chowchilla Grain & Milling Co., my mother took the office manager position so that I could go to college in 1958 (My parents had helped put my sister, my father's daughter from an earlier marriage, through college 13 years earlier). Mother worked six days a week, about nine hours a day at the mill. She prepared three healthful meals a day. She made sure that our family's clothes were clean and ironed. She attended all my school functions to which parents were invited. She made time to listen to me (and always responded with a subtle humor and a heart for the "underdog," like the girl who called and asked to come to our house one afternoon).

My mother loved me.

Over the years

I began to understand why Florence Shobe was "Mother," not "Mom" or "Mama."

I began to notice how "Pinky," my mother's mother, Mamie Garrison, greeted my mother. Never a hug, never a kiss, never an "I love you." However, when Pinky came to our house for a week every summer, supposedly just for a visit, she cleaned and organized every cupboard in the kitchen, fixed all the meals, and did the dishes with me so that my mother and father could get some rest.

I never knew my grandfather, Lawrence Garrison. He had contracted tuberculosis, a dreaded contagious disease without a cure, during the Mexican Border War (1910-1919), and became very ill during my mother's elementary and high school years. After he spent several months in a TB sanitarium, my grandmother brought him home to Ceres, California, and prepared an "isolation" room for him at the back of their home, prepared three good meals a day, boiled every dish from which my grandfather ate, and kept an immaculate house while taking care of their four small children (born 1910, 1912, 1914 and 1918). In those days, of course, dishwashers, washing machines and "baby-sitting" televisions were far into the future. (After I had two children of my own 14 months apart and was feeling a bit overwhelmed and exhausted by the work needed to take care of them, I asked my grandmother, "Pinky, how did you do it?" "I just DID," she answered.

Why did my mother subtly chastise me for not wanting to invite to our home the girl who had called? Why did she ALWAYS pull for the underdog? Many people uneducated about tuberculosis in the early 1900s considered the disease "dirty" and shunned the family taking care of one struck by it. My mother, her brother and sisters seldom were allowed to ask schoolmates to their house to play and rarely were invited to other homes in the small town in which they lived. During one of our talks, Mother told me that during her high school years (when her mother had prepared the home so that guests could come and not come in contact with the dread disease), she had invited a friend to spend the night. The invited girl was having a wonderful time with Mother's family until her own mother rang the doorbell, blasted my grandmother with "If I had known you had TB in your home, I never would have allowed my daughter to be here" and jerked the girl out of the house.

My mother was humiliated.

The Garrison family was well known in Ceres. My great-grandparents owned the meat market and a large home on one of the main streets. Therefore, even though many people feared my grandfather's disease, they let the family know that they still were respected and accepted. My mother was popular at her schools. She held offices in school classes and clubs, played on the school's tennis team, and became a star stenography student. And when my grandfather died in 1931, she and the rest of her family learned something about Ceres, California, as a caring village. "He had one of the biggest funerals ever seen in Ceres," she told me. "People came from Modesto, as well as Ceres. They loved him." Also, either before or after my grandfather died, the city of Ceres named a street, Lawrence Street, for him. Garrison Street, another Ceres street, too, was named for my mother's family.

Later, Pinky, in her early 70s in 1961 and living in a Berkeley, California, apartment, was diagnosed with inoperable pelvic cancer and given six months to live. When the doctor gave her the news, she did not cry nor complain. She merely replied, "No, I am not ready to go yet." She insisted on moving back to her apartment, ate many good vegetables, forced herself to walk a block farther each week and began to get well. She lived to age 91.

That stoicism was passed on to my mother. I saw my mother cry only once. She had sat on a hornet.

While I was in the eighth grade, Mother, age 42 in 1954, was diagnosed with corneal dystrophy. She was told she was going blind and that no cure was possible (Later, in 1958, Dr. Max Fine, a San Francisco ophthalmologist, restored her sight with two medically innovating corneal transplants). During the four years she was losing her sight, she never questioned "Why me?" and very few people knew she was losing her sight. She also taught me to tell her who was approaching as we walked down the street so she would not appear unfriendly. She lost her driver's license and never could drive again. This must have been very difficult for a woman who got her first license and bought a car in her early 20s and then drove across country to Washington, D.C., to work at the Department of Interior for a year before returning to Modesto to marry my

18

father. However, she never complained about the consequences of going blind. When my father or a friend was not available to give her a ride to a local appointment, she walked there.

Many years later, on Thanksgiving Day 1981, I had recently separated from my husband and, although my children and I were living in Granite Bay, California, I was driving my parents, my young son and daughter back to Chowchilla after spending the day with my sister's family in Santa Clara, California. An unlicensed driver in a car with bald tires skidded on the wet, two-lane Highway 152 and hit our car so hard we screeched to a stop just before rolling down a steep hill. My father, age 83, lived a few weeks in a semi-coma before dying. My mother had moved between my children in the back seat a few minutes before the accident. When she saw the other car skidding toward us, she threw both her arms around my children to hold them tightly upon impact. She then was thrown across the console in the front seat, resulting in her suffering two broken arms and two broken legs. My children, because of my mother's quick actions, had minor physical injuries. I suffered only major bruises and a sprained ankle from riding the brake into the crash.

After an ambulance took us to the Gilroy hospital, my father, who had hit his head on the car's glove department button and had suffered broken ribs from the tightening of his seatbelt, was placed in a regular private room. Mother, then age 69, was taken to Intensive Care, where she was in a semi-coma and scheduled for surgery the next morning to set her broken bones as soon as an operating room could be ready. The doctor planned to mold her arms and legs back together (using something like "silly putty," he said). Because my mother's blood pressure was extremely low, though, the doctor told me she probably would not live through the night.

Obviously, that doctor did not know my mother. She lived through the night, survived the long surgery, and endured the 170-mile ambulance transfer with my father (who was almost comatose by then) to her long stay at a hospital near my home, Roseville Community Hospital, where she stayed several weeks. My father sank deeper and deeper into a coma and revived only a moment on Christmas Day, when they wheeled him in to be with my mother. With a trembling hand, he reached up and placed it on my mother's casted arm.

The night I got the call that my father, now age 84, had not survived the severe blows to his body, I told the doctor that I wanted to be the one to tell my mother. She adored my father, as he adored her, and somehow I knew that she would want to hear about his death from me, not a doctor.

When I walked into Mother's room that evening, she knew something was wrong because I had left the hospital for the day about two hours before.

"It's Daddy, isn't it? she asked. No tears, no scream, only a steely look of determination that she COULD and WOULD handle his death. She still was very weak and not able to go to his memorial service.

After her stay at Roseville Community Hospital, she spent nearly two months convalescing under the care of my children and me at our home. Still suffering from the effects of broken arms and legs, yet determined to walk again, she faithfully did all the painful exercises her physical therapist assigned her.

When my mother was first brought to our house after her hospitalization, she could not be left alone. Both her legs and both her arms were still in casts, and she could not get out of bed by herself. She had a hospital bed and a telephone on a stand by her bed. One morning, assured that she would be fine for about an hour, I left to get my hair cut. When I returned home from the salon and walked into my mother's room, my mother said, "The Chowchilla Convalescent Hospital called while you were gone. Mother (Pinky) is dying. I need to go down there right now."

"There's no way you can go there, Mother. " I told her. "First of all, I can't get you into the car, and, secondly, you are not strong enough yet to go."

"Well," she said, "Either you will take me, or I will call a cab."

I called our neighbor, Basil Burnstad, and asked him to help me get Mother into my car. Thank God he was a big, strong man. I then drove very fast down Highway 99, not knowing whether Pinky still would be alive when we got there. Mother said very few words all the way south.

When we arrived at the hospital and I walked up to the director's office, Ellie Brown, the director, knowing our situation, grabbed a couple of orderlies to rush a wheelchair to our car and then accompanied my mother and me to my grandmother's bedside.

When my mother saw my grandmother, there were no words of love, no tears.

"You know why I haven't been here, don't you, Mother?" my mother asked Pinky. Pinky answered, "Yes." "And you know about Clifford?" "Yes." Pinky then turned her head away and died a short time after.

"Your grandmother knew that your mother was coming (I had called the hospital to learn my grandmother's condition), and she waited for her to get here." Ellie Brown told me. "I've seen that before."

Pinky needed to know before she died that my mother would be all right. She also knew that if she died before my mother was there to be with her, my mother would never forget it.

My grandmother loved my mother.

After a few months at our home, Mother announced that she was going back to live in her home in Chowchilla. No amount of my pleading and asking her to be reasonable could dissuade her.

"If the doctor says I am able to go home, will you take me?" she asked. Knowing that her orthopedic surgeon never would agree with her that living alone yet was reasonable, I agreed to her proposal. She set up a visit to the doctor. I explained to the doctor that she would be living alone, walking rather clumsily on a walker and could not prepare good meals for herself.

Then, my mother, in a voice that revealed who truly was in charge of the office visit, said, "I will have my cleaning lady come once a week, and I have many friends who will look out for me."

"I see no reason why your mother can't go home," the doctor said.

Was he kidding? Was the man certifiably nuts?

My question may not have been very far off. A few months after my mother returned home, she was walking on her walker down Robertson Boulevard when she fell down a curb and broke her hip. By this time, she was 70 years old. This is it, I thought. Now she probably will be in a convalescent hospital for the rest of her life. What 70-year-old can survive two broken arms, two broken legs and a broken hip within about six months and recover enough to live independently?

My mother.

Again, I tried to reason with her, and again she parried with the "If the doctor says" proposal. This time I knew I was safe. NO doctor would agree that she was strong enough to live alone and take care of herself.

Wrong again. I do not know how much she might have "offered under the table," but she found a Chowchilla doctor (not one who lived in town but one who came from the Bay Area once a week for a few office hours) to back her up.

I am sure that many people in Chowchilla were appalled that I would allow her to live alone again. However, I knew that her close friends, people who really knew her, would "get it." And they did. They set up a schedule so that each day of the week was covered by a visit from a friend. Mother loved that they enjoyed her "social hour" with her,

Mother lived in her home in Chowchilla another 18 years before she became so frail, at age 88, that the gig was up. She had fallen a few times, she was not eating and was down to about 96 pounds.

However, the gig was not up for her. "I am getting things ready so that I can move," she would respond when I told her that I had found an excellent assisted-living place in Roseville, near my home, "but I need to go through some things first." Honestly, because she was my mother, I initially believed her. And then when I would drive down to Chowchilla to visit her, I began to see that nothing had changed – except her. She was becoming even more frail.

I also was beginning to "get" why she was "not ready" to sell her house and move into a $4,000-a-month assisted living facility (I was working full time and could not care for her in my home). "You don't know how to manage money, Dianne. You don't even clip coupons." (Remember, she had been the office manager at the feed mill).

So that was it. My mother knew she could handle a change in her life. However, she was worried that she would go through all her money, that I would have to pay part of her assisted-living costs and no money would be left to help take care of me after she was gone and no money to leave my sister and her family.

Eventually, my daughter and I moved her into Fountainwood, a beautiful, caring facility in Orangevale, near Granite Bay. Mother then informed me that she was going to call a lawyer and sue me for moving her there. She also demanded to see all her bills before I paid them. However, one day she let me know in a small way that she forgave me for moving her there. She said that when she arrived at the breakfast table an hour early one morning, she laughingly told one of the nurses, "Now I'm beginning to understand why my daughter moved me into here."

She died at Fountainwood less than a month before her 90th birthday

At Mother's memorial service at the former First Presbyterian Church in Chowchilla, I stood at the pulpit and thanked the more-than-150 friends, young and old, for taking care of her during her last years in Chowchilla and for coming to her service. "I'm sure you are all aware that my mother never wanted to leave Chowchilla," I said. Knowing how hard my mother fought me when I tried to move her from her home in Chowchilla, her friends broke into loud laughter.

They loved and admired my mother.

So did I.

Memory Snapshot # 4: My father, in his 60s, on the top rung of a ladder, leaning over our Robertson Boulevard home's garage and trying to coax down Scooter, our cat.

"That Damn Cat"
My father, Clifford Evin Shobe

My father: "That DAMN CAT is on the garage again, and he's so dumb he keeps backing up every time I reach out to grab him."

My mother: "You're going to fall off that ladder. Why don't you just leave him up there?"

My father: "He's scared."

**My father,
Clifford Shobe
1897-1982**

**Scooter
"That damn cat"**

Over the years

While my mother was "Mother," my father was always "Daddy." He could be stern and demanding, but he was always "Daddy." If my father had answered the phone when my high school classmate called, he immediately would have invited her over and, before she arrived, had a long talk with me about doing "the right thing," about kindness, about treating people with respect. He would have acknowledged my hesitation about inviting her for the afternoon and probably told me a story about how he had felt that way at times over the years. He would have ended our talk with a hug and "I know you will want to do the 'right thing.'"

I know that my father was not a "model youth." He was reprimanded by his principal, Thomas Downey, for smoking a cigarette at Modesto High School, he dropped out of high school at age 16, he was known for frequenting a bar in Escalon, a small town near Modesto, when he was in his 20s and 30s, he ignored his mother's urging to attend church, and he had a "hush-hush" experience with a young French woman while he served in Bordeaux, France, during World War I.

A few months after my family moved from Modesto to Chowchilla in 1947 and my parents had built a small brick garage house on Sonoma Street to be our "temporary" home (We did not move into our Robertson Boulevard house until 1957), I had a severe attack of appendicitis. My father had gone hunting with a few of the men he had met in our new town, and my mother was alone until after midnight to deal with a daughter crying in pain. My mother had no car, and a telephone had yet to be installed. She was not amused when she learned that night that the hunters had taken a detour to a bar on the route home.

That was the "wild" side of my father. My son, in a high school English essay, reveals the man who was respected and loved by his family and his community:

"Grandpa,"
By Jonathan Lederer

It was a day I will never forget. My family and I drove down to my aunt and uncle's house for Thanksgiving dinner. We ate and enjoyed our relatives' company for a long time before we all decided it was time to

26

leave. My grandparents joined us on the fateful car ride home. On the way to my grandparents' house, a light rain began to fall. We were driving through a mountainous pass and the conditions became somewhat difficult. All of a sudden a car lost control and impeded the progress of our car. Impact was unavoidable and the two cars slammed together violently.

It is never a pleasant experience to lose a family member, especially while one is young. I had just turned nine when we received the call saying that my grandfather had died from injuries he sustained in the accident. I didn't have many memories of my grandpa while he was alive. I was young and only knew him to be the man I would see when we went down to visit him and my grandmother. I had no idea about the tremendous impact that he had on the local community. I didn't know how many people there were who respected him as an honest and loyal friend and businessman.

It wasn't until his funeral that I was introduced to the fact that he was loved by many people in the town in which he lived. At the funeral chapel, there was room for many people to pay their last respects. However, there wasn't enough room at my grandfather's funeral. The chapel was packed and it was standing room only because he had so many friends and associates.

As years went by, I began to hear stories about my grandpa that made me respect him enormously. Friends of his and my grandma would tell me about how he was the most honest businessman they had ever dealt with and how they will never forget how much they admired his honesty. I later found out that he was the recipient of the Paul Harris Award, which is the highest honor that one can achieve as a Rotarian. Another thing I learned was that he always gave to people in time of need and was kind. He owned a feed mill right on the main railroad and constantly had hobos come into his mill and ask him to lend them a hand. He always gave them enough money to pay for a meal and although they always told him they would pay him back, he never received a penny in return.

Losing a grandpa to a car accident was a very painful experience for me, but as I grow older and see what kind of man he was while he was living, it makes me respect him even more. After seeing how he affected people and how they loved and admired him, it makes me want to become more like he was. Traits such as honesty and kindness that he had are things I hope people respect me for. I would be completely satisfied with myself if I could have as much positive impact on my community as he had on his."

The Bluebird Girls float in the Chowchilla Festival Parade in the late 1940s. I am the second girl from the left in the front row.

Memory Snapshot #5: Riding on a float in the parade down Robertson Boulevard during the Chowchilla Fair and Festival

"I alone cannot change the world, but I can cast a stone across the water to create many ripples."

Mother Teresa

No viewers of the annual festival parade down Chowchilla's palm-lined main street during the 1940s and 1950s had a smart phone, and probably not a video camera, to capture on film the parade entries as they passed by. However, the onlookers during those decades would have seen what made Chowchilla the village that prepared a host of children for the adulthood they would face, either in a small town or a big city:

*The parade Grand Marshals, honored for their service to the community, riding in the lead car and waving and calling greetings to the onlookers.

*The Chowchilla Union High School Band, about 100 strong, in the red and white uniforms and shako hats the community had held fundraisers to buy. The band was led by a drum major and baton-tossing majorettes. Community members and groups took pride in the band, helped the band raise money for our annual trip to the All-Western Band Review in Long Beach and for bus rides to our performances at out-of-town football games and parades.

Also in the parade were bands representing Chowchilla elementary schools. The two I remember from years ago were the excellent Wilson and Dairyland school bands. (Many years after I had moved away from Chowchilla, I was the testing administrator at a large charter school in the San Juan Unified School District, based in Carmichael, California. I had been on the same staff with one of the about 200 teachers a few years when I mentioned that the Rev. Archie Marston had been my pastor years before. "Archie Marston was my pastor too," she said. When I responded that she must have grown up in Stockton, where the pastor served after leaving Chowchilla, she said, "No, he was my pastor in a little town called Chowchilla." And when she told me her maiden name, Helene Ripley, I remembered her as a little girl in Sunday School when I was a teenager. I also remembered that her father, Dick Ripley, had been the director of the Dairyland elementary school band.)

Several high school and elementary school bands from other towns and cities were annual participants in the parade. Merced High School, probably the only high school in Merced at the time, was always a favorite to win the overall band award. The marching "orange and black" was a frequent sweepstakes winner in the parade band division. The Chowchilla band was not eligible for awards because it was the host band.

This photo was taken of the Western pit-style barbecue serving line at the Fairgrounds back in 1948. Identified as the servers are Don Crocker and the late Ralph Lynd, and in the foreground, Lowell Beers. Across the line, getting their share of the "vittles" are Florence and Cliff Shobe. Of course, we are only guessing - are we right?

This was a Looking Back feature of the *Chowchilla News*.

*Throughout the parade were floats representing Chowchilla's youth groups. I remember riding on the Bluebirds, Camp Fire Girls and Job's Daughters floats. Other groups represented, as I recall, were the Boy Scouts, DeMolays and Rainbow Girls. Usually some of the members' fathers and sons built the foundations for the floats, and the mothers and girls decorated them. Many Chowchilla parents and other adults were leaders of youth groups, camp organizers and counselors, and financial supporters.

*Always welcome were the majestic horses and their proud riders atop jeweled saddles. The horses seemed to know they were "on parade," and an onlooker with a good imagination might swear that the equines stopped a second, turned and bowed to their audiences.

*Also represented on floats or in decorated cars were the Chowchilla Fire Department, City Council, and other city groups; service clubs; and the Veterans of Foreign Wars.

Following the parade was the annual beef barbecue at the Madera County Fairgrounds, located, of course, in Chowchilla. People, many of whom were former residents of Chowchilla, drove for miles to stand in lines for the delicious shredded barbecued beef, the beans and the salad.

Over the years

The children who grew up in Chowchilla's supportive "village" became parts of new villages as they branched out into colleges, the workforce and new communities.

*Members of Bluebirds, Camp Fire Girls, Cub Scouts and Boy Scouts and other youth groups saw that many adults in the community used parts of their free time leading the groups; helping with fund-raising projects; transporting children to camps; using their work vacations to set up the camps, serve as camp counselors and cooks, and sit around campfires and listen to the children and give good advice; and good-naturedly become targets of children's pranks. In turn, the children grew up to volunteer at their colleges and new communities so that new generations of children would have the guidance they received in their youth in Chowchilla.

*Members of youth music groups, such as bands and choruses, and youth sports teams learned how long hours of working together as a group resulted in good performances and, often, bringing a trophy back to their hometown. Later, often in new communities, they joined church choirs, community bands and orchestras, adult sports leagues, and service clubs, such as Rotary, Lions, Kiwanis, American Legion, and the Soroptimists\ Club.

*Children saw that the adults in the community worked hard and took pride in their work. Teachers returned homework with comments and helpful suggestions, farmers not only worked from sun-up to sundown but also donated food for community projects, merchants donated their wares as prizes for community and youth fund-raisers. Adults never seemed to be "too tired" to help youths. Young people, as they grew older, carried this same work ethic into their new communities.

*Churches provided Sunday evening youth groups, led by adults. A favorite of teens was the monthly multi-church singspiration, held at various homes in the community, where the host family served homemade cookies and punch. Young people learned the favorite hymns of the churches and later, when life offered challenges, often drew comfort from the memory of a familiar hymn.

*Very few elderly people in the community sat at home alone all day every day. Seniors, who had found friends in school, churches, service groups, and other friend-forming groups in Chowchilla, joined not only in the community's social activities but also in smaller interest groups. For example, my parents belonged to a dinner group that alternated monthly going out to dinner and potluck dinners at members' homes. The group started as a couple's group. However, as one husband or wife died, the remaining spouse continued as a member of the group. I think my mother was the last member of the group to die.

During my first semester at college, I was introduced to my new "village" at the College of the Pacific in Stockton. First, I met a few young women, most from large cities, who lived near me in my dormitory and a few of the young men and women in my classes. And then, another group of Pacific students, some first-year students from small towns, became a part of my social sphere. And it was not by polite introductions.

I was sitting in a large freshman history class taught by Dr. Alonzo Baker, well-known, even nationally, for his witty history lectures. (Not only did Dr. Baker have a local television program, but it was rumored that Mary Baker Eddy, the dynamic founder of Christian Science, once told a young Dr. Baker that he was the only speaker she knew who could hold an audience better than she). Dr. Baker was lecturing our class about the cultural and political climate of California and, before I realized where his lecture was leading, started making fun of small towns.

"It's like one of those little towns down in the San Joaquin Valley — like Coalinga," he said, paused and then with a smirk continued, "Oh no, class, have you ever been to a little town down there called Chowchilla? If you haven't, you've just got to go there." Then he started making fun of my hometown because it was not "cosmopolitan." At this point, my few friends in the class turned to me and started laughing, and the rest of the class caught on that I was from Chowchilla. I was not laughing. My professor was not good-naturedly teasing. He was insulting my hometown.

Dr. Baker quickly caught on. "Oh no," he said, "don't tell me that we have a girl here from Chowchilla."

"Yes, Dr. Baker," I answered, "and I am very proud of that."

"Oh honey," he said. "I am so sorry. I'm so sorry."

After class, several students approached me to tell me that they, too, were from small towns, and they became part of my new village.

Ironically, several years later, my mother called to tell me that she had read in the *Chowchilla News* that Dr. Alonzo Baker and his wife had moved to Chowchilla. (Mother had heard that his daughter lived in Madera and wanted her elderly parents to live not far from her). Of course, during my next trip home I called their home, told Mrs. Baker that I was a former student of Dr. Baker, and asked if I could pay them a visit. She very graciously invited me over. When I asked Dr. Baker if he remembered the young Chowchilla girl in his freshman history class at Pacific, he grinned and said, "I bet you are that girl."

I heard that he died a few years later in the Chowchilla Convalescent Hospital.

I was part of several "villages" during my teaching and newspaper careers, and each village reflected and was benefited by the hometowns of its members. And now, having lived in my home in Granite Bay for 55 years and retired from the workforce for 10 years, I am part of a new village, where I see members giving back to our community the way the people of Chowchilla gave when I was young. Parents coach and help fund-raise for youth groups and sports teams, community members volunteer at food banks and other programs for the homeless, churches and other groups "adopt" refugee families, people with musical talent sing or play an instrument at senior residential homes, people donate money to worthwhile organizations and "come through" when needs arise.

Memory Snapshot #6: A pew in Chowchilla's First Presbyterian Church, about 1977

"He hates sin, but he loves the sinner.'

Dr. Samuel Sutherland, President of the Bible Institute of Los Angeles (now Biola University in La Mirada, California) and son of the Rev. Walter M. Sutherland, speaking at his father's 90th birthday celebration at the Wilson School Auditorium in Chowchilla in 1958

Quote paraphrased from St. Augustine, *Cum dilectione hominum et odio vitiorum,*

"With love for mankind and hatred of sin"

The *Chowchilla News*, 1958, with permission from the McClatchy news corporation. From a family album of Betsy Fry Hofer.

Rev. Walter M. Sutherland, center, is shown here with his sons, Walter Suther-land, left, and Dr. Samuel Sutherland, right, at his 90th birthday party at the Wilson School Auditorium in Chowchilla.

During a weekend visit to my parents' home in Chowchilla when my son and daughter were about 4 and 3 years old, my mother, who was not a church-goer, decided that taking the children to my childhood church, the very conservative (no drinking or smoking) Chowchilla Presbyterian Church, on Sunday was important (Her urging, I suspect, had something to do with her wanting to show off her grandchildren to the congregation, most of whom she knew). Before leaving home for the service, she and I "put the fear of the Lord" into my little son and daughter about behaving in church, especially during the sermon.

The children stood still as the opening hymns were sung, and were very quiet and respectful as the announcements were made, the Scripture read, and the long sermon given. I could see my mother taking her "mental bows" as the people in the pews around us, many of whom were retired elementary schoolteachers, smiled at her in appreciation of her cute and well-behaved grandchildren.

Following the sermon, the ushers passed the Holy Communion bread and grape juice trays down the pews. Because the Presbyterian church, unlike our Evangelical Lutheran Church at home, allowed and encouraged young children to partake of the Communion elements, I whispered to the children that they could take both a piece of the bread and a small glass of grape juice from the trays.

And then, before neither my mother nor I could see what was coming and could stop them, my two children loudly clinked their tiny glasses together and yelled "Cheers!"

Oh my.

My mother, of course, looked as though she were on the verge of a major stroke, and I am sure the scene may have resulted in a few stony stares from a few strict retired schoolteachers. However, as I was quietly explaining to the children that toasting with Communion glasses was not the practice of Christian churches, I could feel, and then hear and see the muffled laughter and loving smiles of nearly all the congregation, a congregation that had "gathered around" the beloved Rev. Walter M. Sutherland for many years.

Rev. Sutherland, born in 1868, was called to the Chowchilla Presbyterian Church in 1931. During his seven years as pastor of the church, he led the church council in building the manse next to the church, the church social hall and the classroom building behind the church. Revealing how much he was respected and loved by the congregation, the church council named the west hall of classrooms Sutherland Hall. The largest room was used mainly for an informal Sunday evening service and Christian Endeavor (the high school group) meetings. Following Rev. Sutherland's retirement as pastor in 1938, he served his later years as pastor emeritus of the church until his death in 1960.

Picture courtesy of Krista Beck,
Rev. Sutherland's great-granddaughter
Rev. Sutherland with his grandson, David, left, and his granddaughter, Beverly, on the front porch of his home on Kings Avenue in Chowchilla.

During his years as pastor emeritus, Rev. Sutherland was relentless in assuring that young people attended the Sunday School class he taught, church services, and Christian Endeavor. He also drove from home to home to give rides to young people whose parents did not drive their children to church. And if a young person was absent from any of these meetings (especially his Sunday School class), the young person could expect a home visit from Rev. Sutherland: "We missed you at church Sunday," he would say. "I hope you were not sick. Will we be seeing you next Sunday? Will you need a ride?"

Church members became increasingly worried about Rev. Sutherland's driving as the pastor aged into his late 80s. And, finally, his driver's license was revoked. His reaction? "But who's going to pick up the young people for church?"

The few Sundays the church's senior pastor was away from the pulpit, Rev. Sutherland was asked to fill in. Fond sighs from the congregation often followed an announcement that he would be preaching because as he aged, his sermons became longer and longer (He must have felt he had less and less time to talk about Jesus). He knew, though, how to handle any sign of restlessness in the congregation, especially the alarm clock hidden in his pulpit one Sunday by some wag. During the service, the alarm sounded loudly at noon, when the service was supposed to end. Rev. Sutherland laughed appreciatively with the congregation and then continued preaching for another 15 minutes.

One Sunday, the congregation was trying desperately not to laugh when the elderly pastor leaned over the pulpit, pointed at the congregation and spoke so emotionally that his top denture flew onto the floor in front of the pulpit. He glanced down, kept on talking, walked around the pulpit, picked up is denture, put it back into his mouth, walked back to the pulpit and continued his sermon without a pause. By this time, however, the congregation could not "hold it together," and Rev. Sutherland had to laugh too as he stopped his sermon for a moment – but just a moment.

After Rev. Sutherland lost his driver's license, he walked to visit as many people in the community as his elderly legs would take him. His visits were not limited to Presbyterians. Even though my parents did not attend church (Their excuse? They kept their feed mill open six days a week, and Sundays were their only days at home), Rev. Sutherland often rang our doorbell. Sometimes he would walk up our front sidewalk about half an hour before dinner time, and my parents ran to hide their "social hour" drinks before greeting him at the front door. When Mother always said, "Rev. Sutherland, you must join us for dinner" he weakly would argue that he "just couldn't stay." However, she easily convinced him that he must. Having him with us was like having a favorite grandfather at our table. He had been widowed a long time, and I know he must have yearned to be with families.

After Rev. Sutherland lost his driver's license, he called my father one hot summer day to tell him that he was going to walk over to the feed mill to visit him and my mother. Of course, my father was not going to let Rev. Sutherland walk across busy Highway 99 in intense heat so he told him that he was just leaving to go into town and would pick him up and bring him to the mill. A few months later, Rev. Sutherland called my father to ask if he "might just happen to be going to Visalia (about 160 miles round trip) that week, that he had an doctor's appointment there (He and my mother had the same eye specialist). My father told him that he had been thinking about driving there to talk with the doctor about my mother's condition and that Rev. Sutherland's eye appointment date would be convenient. On the way to or from Visalia, I imagine that Rev. Sutherland found some way to sneak a subtle lesson about Jesus into the conversation.

During my sophomore year at the University of Pacific in Stockton, my parents called to tell me that Rev. Sutherland had died. They told me that one of the nurses at the hospital where he died told his family that the morning he died he weakly said to the nurse, "I feel sorry for you." When she asked, "Why, Rev. Sutherland?" He smiled and said, "Because today I am going to meet my Savior face to face, and you are going to have to wait awhile."

All Christians who knew Rev. Sutherland were confident that their beloved pastor emeritus had, indeed, met his Savior. We had realized that he would not be with us very much longer, but, still, we deeply felt his loss and the loss of his love and concern for each one of us.

On the Sunday my mother and I took my children to church several years after Rev. Sutherland died, many people in the congregation had been children and teens while he was pastor of the church. And, when the people greeted my children, my mother and me after the service the Sunday we attended, I could feel the warmth and love that he left behind.

I knew that if Rev. Sutherland had still been alive the day we visited my childhood church and if he had heard my children's "toast," he would have knelt beside my children after the service and said something like, "I am so pleased that you children came to church today. Will you come back and see me again?"

Picture courtesy of Leslie Vaughn, Rev. Sutherland's granddaughter.

Rev. Sutherland in the front yard of the Rutherford home on Kings Avenue in Chowchilla (as recalled by Betsy Fry Hofer).

And then, after giving me a hug, he would have said, "Oh my goodness, Dianne, you have beautiful children. And happy children! I LOVE joyful children." And, with a hug and a smile, he would have said, "So does Jesus."

42

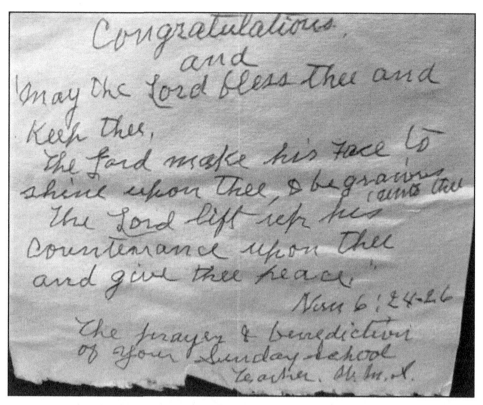

A gift to me from Rev. Sutherland when I graduated from Chowchilla Union High School in 1958. He was 90 years old when he wrote this benediction. I have kept it in my Bible for 59 years.

And to my mother he might have said, "Well, here's the lady who always insists that I stay for dinner. I am so happy that you brought your grandchildren today."

Over the years

Many examples of Christian love are sermons outside the pulpit. People "go the extra mile" to make others feel respected, valued and loved. I have been blessed to have "seen" and "heard" several of those sermons; and, as Edgar A. Guest writes in his poem "*I'd Rather See a Sermon*," "I'd Rather See a Sermon than hear one any day; I'd rather one should walk with me than merely tell the way."

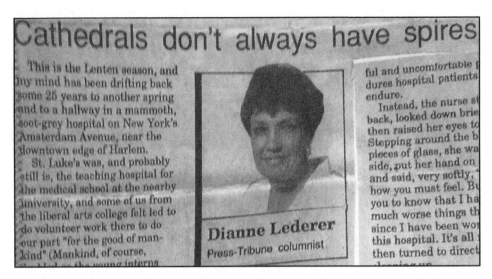

From the *Press-Tribune* in Roseville, California,. Reprinted here with permission from Gold Country Media.

A column I wrote in the 1990s, when I was a copy editor at our local newspaper. The headline was written by the wire editor, Traja Rosenthal.

During the 1990s, when I was a copy editor at my local newspaper, The Press-Tribune in Roseville, California, I wrote a column about one of these "sermons." Another editor, Traja Rosenthal, then the newspaper's wire editor, wrote the headline: "Cathedrals don't always have spires."

Cathedrals Don't Always Have Spires

This is the Lenten season, and my mind has been drifting back some 25 years to another spring and to a hallway in a mammoth, soot-grey hospital on New York's Amsterdam Avenue, near the downtown edge of Harlem.

St. Luke's was, and probably still is, the teaching hospital for the medical school at the nearby university, and some of us from the liberal arts college felt led to do volunteer work there to do our part "for the good of mankind" (Mankind, of course, doubled as the young interns from the university. We also ate dinner a couple of times a week at nearby Union Theological Seminary and made periodic visits to International House Juilliard, a New York music conservatory).

My job at the hospital was to transport cancer patients to radiation therapy and orthopedic cases to physical therapy. As I recall, there were about 12 floors to the hospital, and to this day I secretly believe someone with a perverse sense of humor planned my shifts so that I hit all four corners of the hospital on a floor-rotating basis. (I have to admit at this point that I don't think I missed a window reflection or a mirror on any of those floors as an opportunity to check the fit of my uniform or the state of my hair should I happen to meet a member of the "scrub greens" in the elevator.)

The hospital required that transport volunteers learn several procedures before starting work — how to help a patient into and out of a wheelchair, how to help lift a patient from a bed onto a gurney and back, how to support a walking patient. There also were some lessons in psychology — how to treat patients as people, not cases, and how to listen to patients who know they are dying. And there was the cardinal rule: Unless, responding to an emergency, MOVE SLOWLY. Push wheelchairs slowly, move gurneys slowly, *walk down the halls slowly.*

Obviously the hospital had not taken the time to do a background check on all its volunteers for it would have found that SLOWLY was not a concept in my personal repertoire. I not only moved through life quickly (which did not necessarily equate with well), but I also had very little patience with those who did not.

And, of course it happened. On my way to transport a patient on a very busy morning, I raced into the nurses' station to pick up the patient's chart, rushed out the door, and crashed headlong into a young nurse who was carrying a tray of about 30 blood samples that had just been drawn from an entire wing of patients. The full tubes tumbled from the upended tray, exploded as they hit the floor and splattered blood all across the hallway.

I stood motionless and my face burned with shame as I awaited the angry words that were bound to erupt from one whose profession was a testimony to discipline, one who was acutely aware of the many painful and uncomfortable procedures hospital patients must endure.

Instead, the nurse stepped back, looked down briefly and then raised her eyes to my face. Stepping around the blood and pieces of glass, she walked to my side, put her hand on my arm, and said, very softly, "I know how you must feel, but I want you to know that I have done much worse things than this since I have been working at this hospital. It's all right." She then turned to direct the job of cleaning up.

Two weeks from today the Christian world will be poignantly remembering that centuries ago driven spikes drew other blood -- blood that stained a simple loincloth and trickled down a weathered, rustic cross, and since that time clergy have stood in pulpits around the world to tell about the life and teachings of the lone figure on that cross. But I believe no sermon has ever more powerful than that one brief touch of a hand on my arm.

Memory Snapshot #7: A College Preparatory sophomore English classroom at Chowchilla Union High School in early 1962

"A sense of humor is good for you. Have you ever heard of a laughing hyena with heartburn?"

Bob Hope, comedian, who died in 2003

The sophomores were clever, but I should have been smarter. I should have picked up on the clues.

I had graduated from college midterm and was substitute teaching at a Chowchilla elementary school and at the high school for a semester to make money to help pay for the graduate school I would be attending in the fall. After I had substituted about three weeks, I received a call from Howard Snyder, the high school principal.

"I hate to ask you to do this," he said," but I have a teacher who abruptly resigned and left town because he could not control his English classes. I desperately need a teacher for those classes, and I know you majored in English. Would you be willing to take the job?"

"I will do it," I told the principal. I had known these "rambunctious" students since they were tiny. I had taught some of them in Sunday School, I knew many of their parents, my parents knew many of their parents. Mr. Snyder told me that I would start the next day.

When the school bell began class periods the following day, I told the classes that I knew that they had effectively "run off" their former teacher, reminded them that I had easy access to their parents, and that anything they might think of pulling on me I probably had invented when I had attended that high school just a few years before. They laughed. They had heard stories and knew I was right.

Over the weeks, they continued to listen respectfully while I was talking, they respectfully listened to each other during class discussions, they did their homework. I was proud of myself that I was able to control "uncontrollable" classes.

I was perplexed one day when I saw a note obviously being passed around one of the classes. The note was accompanied by furtive looks and smiles. Obviously, a more seasoned teacher would have interpreted their smiles, demanded the note, pocketed it and read it after class. But, no, I demanded the note, ignored the students' theatric pleas not to take it, opened the folded paper in front of the class and silently read it:

"If you have on red underwear, smile."

OK, you darn kids, that was good.

Over the years

My introduction to the difference between laughing WITH someone and laughing AT someone was in the fifth grade at Monterey School in Chowchilla.

Our afternoon teacher, school principal Carroll Sloper, had served overseas during World War II, and we found that we could divert him from his lesson plans by asking him something about the war. As he was telling us a story one afternoon, he sat on the desk used by both our morning teacher, Ethel Matsel, and by him. He then rose to write on the blackboard.

The class then had a dilemma: Do we laugh or not?

When Mr. Sloper turned back to the class and looked at our faces, he asked what was going on.

"Um, I think you sat in Mrs. Matsel's flower thing," one of the students hesitantly told him.

Mr. Sloper looked at the paint dish filled with water and violets, reached back to feel a wet spot on a strategic place on his pants, smiled, laughed and then said something like, "I guess I am going to have to talk with Mrs. Matsel about where she puts her flowers."

Now we knew we could laugh.

Of course, by the end of the next recess, everyone at the school knew about Mr. Sloper's wet pants. I am sure, also, that his pants were the topic of many Chowchilla dinner tables that night. (Many years later, because I had kept up with Mr. Sloper and his wife, Maxine, over the years, I was invited to Mr. Sloper's 90th birthday party in Winters, California. And three years after that, in 2010, I visited Mr. Sloper in his care home shortly before he died. During my visit, I told one of the caregivers attending Mr. Sloper the story about his "wet pants," and I got to hear his same laugh I had heard 61 years earlier when I was in the fifth grade).

During the rest of our elementary school, high school and college years, my sense of humor rose above the "wet pants" level (Well, maybe not. A Chowchilla family — father, mother and 18-year-old son — took me out to lunch in Washington, D.C., while I was a 1963 summer intern at the Agency for International Development. The mother, son and I laughed uproariously when the father came sheepishly out of the restaurant's men's restroom and seriously tried to explain to us why his pants were sopping wet in front. He kept trying to convince us that the bidet in the men's room had malfunctioned. Of course, the harder he tried to describe how the bidet had "attacked him," the harder we laughed).

Thankfully, from having friends with disabilities, friends of different colors and friends who attended churches much different from Chowchilla's mainstream churches, I learned that jokes about people who seemed "different" in some way were not funny but cruel, and I learned that only when people were laughing WITH someone was teasing fun and appreciated.

I suppose it was inevitable that, as an English major, I would find a way to channel my sense of fun into hopefully clever literary pranks, and my leader into this "prankdom" was a fellow Columbia University graduate student and now published author. She somehow had access to official university stationery, and her friends sometimes received "official" letters from a professor, the president of the university, or the university's board of trustees. She was a master of the craft.

Having been the victim of the "red underwear" prank from my sophomores and knowing my fellow graduate student's talent, I should have known better than to look down and start reading a sheet of paper she had "innocently" slipped over to my desk during Professor Robert Schaffer's lecture in our teaching-methods class. My friend had an unusually good memory and, during the lecture, had rewritten Edgar Allen Poe's "Annabel Lee" as so that it was not about Annabel, but a parody on my life at our school. She had used Poe's rhyming scheme and his meter.

Just as I should have folded the students' note and pocketed it for later reading, I definitely should have quietly folded my friend's paper and put it in my textbook for later reading,. But, no, I glanced down at the paper, could not stop myself from reading it and started laughing so hard that Dr.Schaffer stopped his lecture and asked if I needed to leave class until I could get myself under control. I had literally, all by myself, shut down a class at Columbia University for a while. And my fellow graduate student? During the whole episode, she was the "innocent student" who happened to be sitting by me. She never cracked a smile.

During the year I was at graduate school, Chowchilla High principal Howard Snyder wrote to ask if I would return to Chowchilla High the next year and teach my sophomore class as seniors. Since the requirements for a California Teacher's Credential at that time were either California-based graduate courses I had not taken or a year of teaching, I accepted the senior class English teaching position for a year only.

My former sophomores were now almost two years older. However, some of them were "still my sophomores."

While teaching literature from the Elizabethan Era, I asked the students to create a project that would reflect the era, e.g., find a recipe from the era, prepare the dish and bring enough for the class; build a replica of the Globe Theater; perform a soliloquy from a Shakespearean play; sew an Elizabethan dress; draw a detailed map of London at the time.

When I arrived at school the morning the projects were due, I was summoned to principal Howard Snyder's office.

As I remember his words: "Dianne, can you please tell me why any of your students would be bringing a cannon to school? The police called me this morning. A cop had stopped two of our students because they were driving through town with a cannon on a flatbed truck. The boys explained to the officer that it was for an assignment in Miss Shobe's

English class. The officer called me o find out if that could possibly be true."

About 50 years later, I drove to Chowchilla for the memorial service for one of my late mother's close friends. After the service, a 60-some-years-old man walked up to me, gave me a hug and, with the impish grin I had remembered for more than 50 years, asked, "Do you remember when we drove the cannon into town for your English class?

Yes, I certainly did.

Years after my first teaching assignment, I enjoyed sending "official" letters once in a while to friends I thought would appreciate them (such as a retired kindergarten teacher who, at a Roseville meeting of the American Association of University Women, told of her panties falling down while she was a carrying a Meals on Wheels tray down the street to deliver to a shut-in. She had asked two teenage girls approaching her to hold the tray while she stepped out of her panties and put them in her purse Can you imagine how difficult it must have been for those girls to keep a straight face? I wrote the retired teacher a letter, supposedly from the Fruit of the Loom company, suggesting that if she had been wearing higher-quality panties, such as Fruit of the Loom, she would not have created a scene in downtown Roseville).

It was inevitable, though, that one of my "official" letters would re-sult in a big "Oops" moment. It was at a church choir practice. After a very accomplished choir accompanist at our Lutheran church had moved to another city and an equally accomplished replacement had not been found, one of the choir members, a good friend of mine, knew that I had played the piano when I was very young and finally convinced me that the choir director and choir would be delighted if I would agree to help them out.

"It's very low key," my friend promised. "You don't have to be as good as Karen was. You know a lot of the choir members, and we just have a lot of fun."

The only person I did not know was the choir director. She was the church's organist, director of music and, as I soon learned, a master musician. During my first practice with the choir, she very politely said (in front of the choir), "Dianne, try to use a little less pedal." Then, during the next practices, she repeatedly reminded me (in front of the choir) to go easy on the pedal. Finally, during one practice, her patience had worn thin, and she turned to me (in front of the choir) and said, quite loudly, "Dianne, you MUST stop using so much pedal. The only reason you are using it so much is to try to cover up your mistakes." (The choir, knowing that I never claimed to have concert talent, hesitantly started laughing, but I don't remember the director laughing).

Well now, that outburst from the director definitely called for an "official letter." I asked my computer-savvy daughter to create a template for business stationery and to scatter a few musical notes across the top of the page. For the business name at the top of the page I typed the name and fake New York address of world-famous organist E. Power Biggs. Biggs "supposedly" wrote in the letter to the choir director that he had recently visited friends in Granite Bay and had the opportunity to attend our church, the Lutheran Church of the Resurrection. He commended the director on her organ prelude, noted that the sermon was very good, and wrote that he was particularly impressed with her choir's presentation. "The only thing I would suggest," the letter continued, "is that you ask your pianist to use a little more pedal."

After I ended the letter with "I look forward to my next visit to Granite Bay and your church," I typed the director's address and Biggs' supposed return address on an envelope, stamped the envelope and then mailed the letter in a manila envelope to a New York friend and asked her to drop the letter in the mail so that it would be postmarked from New York.

The choir member who had talked me into playing the piano for the choir was the only choir member in on my prank, and we glanced briefly at each other at the beginning of the next choir practice when we saw that the director had brought a piece of stationery to her music stand.

"I received a letter this week," the director told the choir. She then read the letter, and when she read "The only thing I would suggest is that you ask your pianist to use a little more pedal," I knew I had "scored big" when the choir looked at me and laughed uproariously (They were laughing WITH me).

Again, the director did not laugh. She waited until the laughter died, looked directly at me, looked directly at the choir, and, after a dramatic pause, slowly and firmly said, "Does everyone here know that E. Power Biggs IS DEAD?"

The director got a bigger laugh than my letter. She had "scored bigger."

I started practicing a little more and using less pedal.

Memory Snapshot #8: Walking home from a friend's home

"How we walk with the broken speaks louder than how we sit with the great."

Bill Bennot, <u>Unstoppable Kingdom: An Apostolic Leadership Culture and Transformation</u>

While I was at a friend's home one afternoon, her older brother, about 12 years old, four years older than I and known to be "mean," said to me, "Why don't you go home? You are not wanted here."

Many children, especially those with brothers and sisters with whom to trade regular taunts and insults, would have hurled had an equally rude barb in return and continued playing jacks or whatever other childhood game we were playing. I, though, as an only child in our home with no experience in handling childhood insults, said "OK" and left.

Over the years

That was almost 70 years ago. However, over the last 70 years, "You are not wanted here," said aloud or subtly, to anyone has taken me back to that childhood walk home.

"You are not wanted here," while mostly blatant during childhood, can take silent, often unintended forms in adulthood:

• A person attending a church for the first time stays for the coffee hour, sees cliques of people talking and laughing, but stands uncomfortably alone.

• An elderly person in a care home eagerly watches an entry door to see if a family member or friend has come to visit him or her but sees only greetings and hugs for other residents.

- A new business employee walks into the company lunchroom and sits alone while other employees quickly eat, chat and then run back to their offices.

- An parent is told by an adult child that the child is afraid the parent will eventually become a burden on the child's family.

First Presbyterian Church stationery used during the last half of the 20th century.

#Memory photograph 9: An elderly man sitting on a sofa at Chowchilla's First Presbyterian Church

*"I must remember that every man I meet
is in some way my superior."*

A saying, as I remember on a crossbeam of the Ye Olde Hoosier Inn
restaurant in Stockton

Every day, many hours a day an elderly man in khaki pants, khaki shirt worked in his garden and kept the weeds down at his small wooden house on a corner lot across the street from Chowchilla High School, and almost every Sunday evening he carried his well-worn Bible into a room in the Presbyterian Church's Sutherland Hall and sat on the corner of an old sofa. The man and his wife rarely missed a Sunday Evening Service.

Evening services, attended by about 30 people from teens to the very old, were informal. First a few favorite hymns, a Scripture reading, a short devotional from the pastor and then questions and ideas from the assembled group.

Inevitably, sometime during the discussions, the man raised his large, calloused hand to add something to the discussion that followed. We all knew that the man would take an uncomfortably long time to leaf through the sheer, onion-skin pages of his Bible to find the verse he wanted to add to the conversation. However, we sat quietly and respectfully during the long silence. Eventually he would find his verse and, in a low, barely audible voice, read the verse and then slowly relate its meaning to the topic of the evening.

One Sunday evening, we who attended the evening meetings saw the man raise his hand but did not see him opening his Bible. Instead, he told the group that the Scripture our pastor had raised reminded him of something from Shakespeare. He then recited from memory about 10 lines from one of the bard's plays.

A few years later, after the man's wife died, a daughter moved the man from his little house to a convalescent home near her home in Southern California, and his old house sat vacant for about two years until a fire destroyed it and all the dry vegetation around it. Chowchilla people who remembered the couple said they could still "see" the old man working daily in his garden and were thankful that he was far away and could not see the ruins of his home.

One spring morning a few months later, as I was walking past the charred property on my way to teach English at the high school, I saw that one daffodil, one solitary daffodil, had broken its way through the ashes.

Over the years

Following my 1963-64 year teaching English at Chowchilla High School, I accepted an English-teaching position at Santa Rosa High School in Santa Rosa, California. I was given three sophomore A (college preparatory) classes and two sophomore C (basic) classes.

A tall, strong boy sat quietly at the back of one of my C classes. He spoke only when I addressed him, never raised his hand to ask or answer a question, and did not mix socially with the other students in the class.

Also, he could not read. He could recognize a few small words but could grasp very little of what he was "reading." Occasionally, I believed I had broken through his reading block but soon learned that he had not retained even the most basic lesson I had tried.

In the spring of the school year, in order to add some variety to our daily lessons, I assigned a minimum-three-minute "how-to" speech. "Girls, maybe you like to style hair, " I told the class. "I certainly could use some help with mine. Maybe you could show the class a styling trick. Boys, maybe you like to work with cars. You could save the rest of us a lot of money if you would tell us how to change oil, change a tire, something like that. Just think of something you like to do and are good at and be ready to tell me tomorrow what your topic will be."

I told the class that we would start the speeches in two days and that I wanted them to tell me their topic the next day. The following day, the big boy in the back of the class mumbled, almost inaudibly, that his topic would be "How to Run a Dairy." And then, when I asked who would like to speak first the next day, the big boy raised his hand. I could tell by the class' incredulous looks that they were perplexed. So was I. However, I thanked the boy for volunteering and continued with the day's lesson.

On the day of the speeches, the boy, who had upgraded from his usual jeans and plaid shirt to dressier pants and shirt, took his usual seat until I called on him to give his talk. He walk assuredly to the front of the class, looked seriously at the students and me, picked up a piece of chalk from the blackboard tray and began to speak:

"I am going to talk about how to run a dairy," he said confidently. "There are three grades of dairies, A, B and C." He wrote A,B, can C on the blackboard and then spoke the entire class period on the differences among the dairies and the requirements for operating them. He could have been speaking to an agriculture class at a university. He had not written anything else on the blackboard except A, B and C. He did not need to. And when he put the chalk back into the tray at the end of his talk and the class applauded loudly, he walked nonchalantly back to his seat to pick up his books for the next class.

During the past few years as I have driven to the northern California coast to vacation with family, I have passed through the Santa Rosa countryside and seen large dairy farms. I would not be surprised to learn that the big, quiet boy in my C English class at Santa Rosa High School is the owner of one of the largest. And he probably still cannot read.

Years later in the early 1990s, I received a reminder of the elderly man on the sofa and the boy in my English class. As the Sunday editor of The Press-Tribune newspaper in Roseville, on Saturdays I alone was responsible for the layout, editing, headlines and "putting to bed" of the large Sunday edition. Only one reporter, the photo editor, an assistant photographer and the layout crew worked with me on Saturdays.

One Saturday, after pages were pasted up (this is before computer layouts) shortly before our deadline, I asked the layout people, the reporter, and the photo editor to look over the pages to assure that I had not made a mistake that would be printed and land on readers' porches that Sunday morning. "Looks good to me"-type responses came from all. The reporter, the language expert of the group, had read the pages carefully before declaring them ready for production.

About 15 minutes before deadline, I noticed that the assistant photographer had finished her work for the day. Just to be polite and not leave her out of the proofing group, I asked her to look over the pages.

"Me?" she asked. "I've never done that before."

"Just please make sure the captions are correct under the pictures," I told her.

She walked to the layout tables and slowly began reading the pages. As deadline neared, I became more and more agitated. I really had not needed her to proof for me, I kept thinking, and now she was going to make us miss our deadline.

As she was reading one of the last pages, she turned to me and asked, "Dianne, is this right?"

I smiled confidently and, ready to assure her that the "mistake" she found was not a mistake, walked over to look at the production page.

She had found an English error that would have caused both the newspaper and me major embarrassment had it been printed.

Memory Snapshot No. 10: Receiving a 45 rpm record of my favorite song during lunchtime at Chowchilla Union High School

"A good man does the little things."

From *15 Signs You're With a Good Man*, by James Michael Sama, author and relationship blogger

When I was a senior in high school, the boy I was dating knew that I loved a current hit, "The Shifting, Whispering Sands," by Rusty Draper. Unable to find the record at our local music store, the boy drove to Madera, 17 miles away, during our school's hour lunchtime to buy the hit song for me and drove back to present it to me in a school corridor at the end of the lunch hour.

Over the years

I have dated several men like the boy who bought me the record. They were the men whom I now I see happily celebrating 50th anniversaries with women who fell in love with them and now treasure them. They are usually successful men, not always successful in the money world, but successful in that they have a wife who loves them, children and grandchildren who love them, appreciate them and enjoy spending time with them.

Unfortunately, I always was looking for excitement. During my high school years, I was looking forward to going to college and finding an exciting man there. During graduate school in New York, I dated two Union Theological Seminary students, one "steady" and one "exciting." The steady one would have bought "The Shifting, Whispering Sands" for me. The exciting one talked me into skipping Eleanor Roosevelt's memorial service at St. John the Divine Cathedral near my graduate school in order to "help him with the Sunday sermon" he was going to give at a New York church. "Exciting" turned out to be having me up to his seminary room and expecting something that the church, I am sure, would not have expected as a topic for his sermon.

Eventually in 1969, while I was a high school counselor, I found the excitement I was seeking. I fell in love with the man I had been seeking.

He made me laugh, took me to interesting places, had an interesting job in the space industry and had good, basic values. We married, built a home (in which I am still living), and had a son and a daughter. Unfortunately, after several years, we painfully admitted that we were too different to live with each other, and we divorced. To this day, however, I know that if I were ever seriously in trouble, he would be there for me (He might give me a hard time about how I got into trouble, but he would be there).

And now, in my 70s, I am content with my single life. To combat the "only child" image (My sister is 13 years older than I), my parents brought me up to be very independent, and I always have been self-reliant and have liked making decisions about where I go and how I spend my money. I like living alone with my llasadoodle, Barkley, even though sometimes walking from my car to my house late at night is sometimes a little scary.

Even so, I have to admit that there are times that I envy the young woman who fell in love with and married the boy who drove to Madera and excitedly bought me "The Shifting, Whispering Sands."

Memory Snapshot #11: Listening to Beethoven
on Christmas Eve at a ranch house in Chowchilla

"The fresh and crisp air of the country reminds me that our blood surges from of the natural world and how tied we are to the sprung rhythms of earth and sky, weather and season."

Kilroy J. Oldster, Dead Toad Scrolls

The Chowchilla ranchers and farmers who bought feed for their animals and seeds for their crops at the Chowchilla Grain & Milling Co., where my father was manager and my mother office manager and my parents part-owners, became good friends of my parents. One family, the Witesmans, invited my parents and me for a clam chowder dinner every Christmas Eve. When I was very young, I did not appreciate the tradition because all I wanted to do was stay home and open the presents around our Christmas tree. However, as I grew older, I began to treasure the ranch house dinner, the ranch house library filled with classics and first-editions, the classical music that came from a phonograph near the bellow-fanned fire in the small rock fireplace and the homemade fruit pie served near the end of our visit.

Over the years

From the time I was a little girl, I considered "the mill," the Chowchilla Grain & Milling Co., my family's mill, even though my parents were only part-owners. Instead of going to day care after school days ended, I spent late afternoons at the mill. I learned to candle eggs so that I could spend time in the ice-cold candling room during the hot San Joaquin Valley summers. I loved to run my hands through the bins of barley and milo. I slid down the feed-sack chutes despite my father's

Elwyn Feaver, field man at the CHOWCHILLA GRAIN & MILLING CO., demonstrates the high quality feed to David Serrano and Dick Evans.

George Wessels Photography, 1958 La Entrada

A Chowchilla Grain & Milling Co. advertisement in the 1958 La Entrada, the Chowchilla Union High School yearbook.

admonitions that they were dangerous. I helped myself to the soft drinks in the ice-cold cooler with the lift-up lid. And I spent great deal of my time getting to know — pestering is probably the more accurate term — the workers at the mill and the ranchers and farmers who brought in their crops and came to load their trucks with bags of feed.

The people I met at the mill were a major part of our small agricultural community, and these people created the images I now consider priceless gifts. For I always have preferred a laughter-filled, hot-biscuit breakfast or fried chicken dinner around an old ranch table over a cocktail party that requires "small talk." My love for classical music comes Christmas Eves spent at a ranch house. And I admire the kind of judgment it takes to rotate crops wisely and make maximum use of land far more than the judgment required to make money for money's sake. I also understand the financial devastation crop-growers feel when storms or droughts destroy their crops.

Store-bought desserts just do not cut it after I have spent time in the large ranch kitchens of women who made pie crusts with lard. The women also made preserves, sewed smart-looking clothes, gardened, kept up with the world and still found time to be loving wives, mothers, friends. And, I have to admit, I always will be partial to the strong, yet gentle men in the dusty flannel shirts.

They tore the old mill down long ago, and a freeway bypass and Shell service station have taken its place. I was not devastated by the progress represented by the crumbled bricks. And yet, every time I drive into my hometown, I always will see the image of a massive building rising above the yellow service station sign.

Memory Snapshot #12: A dream of the future

"Two Roads Diverged in a Yellow Wood;
I took the one less traveled by,
And that has made all the difference."

From "The Road Not Taken," by Robert Frost

During my childhood and teen years, I had a vague impression of how my life would unfold: I would go to college, become a high school English teacher, marry my "soulmate" (preferably an exciting church minister), have two children, live in a wooded area in California, have many friends, travel to interesting places, celebrate our Golden Wedding anniversary, be surrounded in my old age by my husband, children and grandchildren, live to my late 90s as my paternal forebears lived and be buried beside my husband in our hometown, wherever that might be.

Over the years

I, of course, have no idea how many more years I will live. My mother died at age 89, my maternal grandmother at age 91, my paternal grandmother at age 96. However, I do know that during the years I have left, I probably will not change very much. I hope to continue to grow and learn, but I will continue to be a combination of my heredity and the lessons I have learned over the years. Those lessons began in my home and in the small 1940s-50s town of Chowchilla, California:

*Today my first inclination at a social gathering is to look for people I know, but thank you to my late friend Nicky for making me feel welcome my first day in a second-grade class. Many years later, about 45 years ago, one of our new neighbors in the area where we had recently built our home in Granite Bay asked her pastor, Pastor Paul Carlson of

Resurrection Lutheran Church in Granite Bay, to visit me in Roseville Hospital after I had unexpected surgery. He visited me every day I was in the hospital and then visited us in our home several times while I recovered at home. My neighbor had become my new community "Nicky," and, of course, I joined Resurrection Lutheran because of the pastor's care, concern and prayers. Over the years I have seen and sometimes been a part of the care and love our church members have shown not only members and guests, but also the community at large. "All are welcome at our Lord's table," our pastors tell the congregation during Sunday services, and ALL people are welcome at our church. Also, I am thankful for the many friends I have made over the years and am especially grateful as I grow older and realize that friends are blessings.

*Today I am quite confident in my God-given abilities. However, thank you to Mr. Stephens, director of my high school band, I have learned that I am not the best I can be and that I must not stop learning and improving.

*Today my faith is the foundation of my life, but thank you to my mother for reminding me that having faith without treating other people with kindness and respect does not honor God and for teaching me, by her example, that love is shown in many different ways.

*Today I sometimes I get upset by minor annoyances (e.g., far too many "ums" in people's conversations), but thank you to my father for his example of looking past annoyances and showing tolerance and kindness (I am still working on that one). Also, today I have Barkley, a wonderful llasadoodle. I know if my father were still alive, Barkley would have another name too, "That damn dog," but my father always would have a doggie treat in his hand when Barkley arrived in Chowchilla.

*Today I give back to my community in only a few small ways, but thank you for the examples of the men and women who gave their time and talents to the youths and other community groups. The examples from my youth have given me an awareness and appreciation of what many of my friends and acquaintances do today for our community.

From the photo collection of Pastor Ralph Supper

One of our pastors, Pastor Ralph Supper of the Lutheran Church of the Resurrection in Granite Bay, California, offers Communion to travelers along Douglas Boulevard to send the message that God loves them and that they are welcome to worship with us at our church.

Barkley

*Today, I have to admit, I love playing bingo and slot machines, as well as enjoying a good Cosmopolitan martini with friends, but, because of Rev. Sutherland and others at the First Presbyterian Church, I also had examples of the love Christ taught. I am still struggling to understand how to reconcile my enjoyment of what some may think of as sins and my faith in Jesus Christ, but occasionally I see a glimmer of how they might serve together (even though I know that people might think that I am merely trying to justify my jackpots and Cosmos). Today I am attracted to people with a quick wit and enjoy many types of humor, but thank you, Mr. Sloper and my former Chowchilla students, for teaching by example the difference between laughing at someone and laughing with that person.

*Today I sometimes tempted to make a quick judgment about a person because of how the person looks, what the person says or where the person works;

but thank you to the man on the sofa at Chowchilla's First Presbyterian Church for teaching me that "a quote from Shakespeare" might be hidden in that person's heart.

This banner, created by church member Josie Freiberg, proclaims that our church, the Lutheran Church of the Resurrection in Granite Bay, California welcomes and embraces ALL people.

*Today I sometimes am not "drawn to" a person and my first instinct is to retreat; but thank you to my childhood neighbor boy who, unknowingly, taught me the devastating feeling of not being wanted.

*Today I still am attracted to "exciting men," but thank you to my high school boyfriend for showing me a quality that is much more important than excitement.

Finally, thank you, to all the people I have known in Chowchilla, California, who made the little town I grew up in a place I am very proud to call my hometown.

And -- Cheers!

History of Chowchilla

From the City of Chowchilla Web Site

Some of the information that follows comes from the compilation book titled, "Yesterdays of Chowchilla" last published in 1991 by the then Chowchilla Historical Society. The book has not been updated since then and known copies exist at the public library, chamber of commerce office, city hall and perhaps other locations. It is unknown if copies of the book can be obtained from any source. As possible this page will be updated with additional reference information and web links.

Founding of Chowchilla

Chowchilla's colorful past began in the spring of 1844 when John Fremont and his party were making their way across what is now Madera County.

In Fremont's memoirs we find the following recording: "Continuing along we came upon broad and deeply-worn trails which had been freshly traveled by large bands of horses, apparently coming from the San Joaquin Valley. But we heard enough to know that they came from the settlements on the coast. These and indications from horse bones dragged about by wild animals - wolves or bears - warned us that we were approaching the villages of Horse-thief Indians, a party of whom had just returned from a successful raid." This brief mention of the "Horse-thief Indians" gives us an introduction through the eyes of the white man, of the early inhabitants of the Chowchilla area.

Chowchilla Tribe

The Chowchilla Indians lived along the several channels of the Chowchilla River in the plains region of Central California. According to one authority, the Chowchilla tribe may well have been a very populous tribe. At least we know they were a warlike one and the name Chowchilla was a byword for bravery to the southernmost end of Yokuts territory in the southern end of the San Joaquin Valley.

The growth of the Chowchilla area and subsequent development of the town does not need such fiction to make a thrilling but true story. From the days of the "Killer Indians" and the struggles of the early pioneering families to the dreams of O. A. Robertson, we have all the color and romance a student of history needs.

Orlando Alison Robertson

Mr. Orlando Alison Robertson was born in Prosperity, Pennsylvania on August 18, 1858. Having lost his mother when only a small child, he was raised by an aunt on a farm near the place of his birth. By thrift and hard work, he managed to secure an education, finally graduating from the California Normal School at California, Pennsylvania.

Not long after Mr. Robertson graduated from college, he married Miss Frances Mackey of Pittsburgh. They moved soon after to Campbell, Minnesota where Robertson taught public school. He also engaged in farming and real estate. In time, he became the County Superintendent of Schools in the Red River Valley of western Minnesota.

Robertson saw the possibilities in land speculation and gathered the financial backing of several men in the community. He began to buy large tracts of Northern Pacific Railroad land at ninety-nine cents an acre. This group of men was called the First Minnesota Land and Colonization Company, and altogether they purchased over a million acres of land in Minnesota, the Dakotas, Colorado, Utah, Oregon, California and in two of the three provinces of Canada. They also purchased extensive coal mining properties in England and had lumbering interests in British Columbia and Saskatchewan.

Early 1990s

Around 1910, Robertson became interested in land development in California. It was during that year he organized the United States Farm Land Company. He established a general office in Sacramento and maintained offices in Winnipeg, St. Paul and Denver.

At the time Robertson became interested in the Chowchilla area, he was estimated to be worth over four million dollars. Those who knew him described him as a man of compelling personality and boundless energy. Though he was a man of sound integrity, he was also something of a philosopher and dreamer. Robertson believed that Chowchilla was ready for immediate development and held ambitious hopes for transforming the land into prosperous farms owned by happy people. He put all his money into the Chowchilla venture against the advice of his financial counselors and, as we shall see, it cost him heavily.

On May 22, 1912, Robertson purchased the Chowchilla Ranch from the California Pastoral and Agricultural Company Ltd. Over half of this ranch was divided into tracts for sale to farmers and the northeast corner of the property was set aside for the site of the town which became known as Chowchilla.

Robertson's ambitious plans were soon carried out. Surveys were completed and maps were made. Streets in the town site and about 300 miles of country roads were opened. This included the 12 mile palm tree lined Robertson Boulevard. A large hotel and office buildings were erected. Soon, a town water system was put into operation and streetlights were put up. Later, some 12 miles of railroad (now abandoned) was laid in connection with the Southern Pacific Line. The purpose of the railroad was to aid settlers and expedite the new colonizing efforts.

Colonization Project

October 15, 1912 was the date set for the grand opening of the colonization project. An extensive advertising program had been conducted and on that date some 4,000 people responded to the invitation to look over the new land, see the rodeo and partake of the free barbecue lunch at noon. The day was hot and dry, and according to those present, the beans were salty, causing many to drift to Tom's Saloon at Minturn (six miles north) to slack their thirst. October 15, 1912 is still remembered as the day Minturn went dry.

In 1917, Louis Swift, a Chicago packer, and Robertson purchased the Western Meat Ranch which was roughly 40,000 acres of adjoining property. It has since then been operated as a cattle and farming operation under different managements. Then in 1919, Robertson purchased 26,000 acres of the Old Bliss Ranch. The land was again subdivided and sold in small tracts.

Robertson had much of his money tied up in extensive land speculation ventures, and when the country began to experience the recession and subsequent Great Depression of the late 20's and early 30's, he became more and more pressed for funds. When Robertson passed away on May 23, 1933, he had lost his vast fortune and died practically penniless.

Community Growth

Though Chowchilla lies in the center of California and beside the main lines of the Southern Pacific, it was not the outgrowth of a geographic or economic need. It was, in fact, the result of the thinking and planning of one man: O. A. Robertson. The Chowchilla colonization project was not unique in California's history. Other small communities such as Kerman, Wasco, Shafter, Patterson, Oakdale and Laguna de Tache were all the products of such private land company efforts. But taken collectively, they are a part of a unique story; the story of a group of farsighted real estate promoters who saw the future and agricultural productivity of this Valley.

Made in United States
Orlando, FL
24 October 2022

23803592R00046